Sonder

Manasi Jare

BookLeaf Publishing

India | USA | UK

Presentation by *BookLeaf Publishing*

Web: www.bookleafpub.com

E-mail: info@bookleafpub.com

ISBN: 9789360947590

First edition 2024

*To every memory and every heart, shaping me
into the story I am.*

ACKNOWLEDGEMENT

As I reflect on the journey that led to the creation of *Sonder*, I am filled with gratitude for the many individuals who have supported and inspired me along the way.

First and foremost, I would like to express my deepest appreciation to my family and friends for their unwavering love, encouragement, and belief in my creative endeavors.

To my mentors and teachers, whose wisdom and guidance have shaped me as a poet, I am forever grateful.

To my readers, whose curiosity and open hearts have welcomed *Sonder* into the world, thank you for embarking on this poetic journey with me.

Lastly, I dedicate *Sonder* to the countless strangers whose lives intersect in the pages of this book. May we continue to find solace, understanding, and empathy in the shared moments of our collective journey.

With deepest gratitude,
Manasi

PREFACE

In the vast expanse of existence, we are but fleeting moments in the lives of others, intersecting briefly on the journey of our shared humanity. In *Sonder*, traverse the landscape of human experience, from the depths of despair to the heights of joy. These poems capture the essence of what it means to be alive, to love, to grieve, and to find solace in the beauty of the world around us. As you embark on this journey through *Sonder*, may you find resonance in these verses and discover the profound beauty of the human experience.

Petals and Pictures

After summer's slumber, flowers bloom anew,
Gone is the scorching sun, replaced by skies of
blue.
Valleys burst with colors, a vibrant sight to
behold,
In my hometown, a carpet of petals unfolds.

Red, white, pink, yellow, purple hues,
Nature's palette, a breathtaking muse.
Grasses sway green, windmills tall and proud,
In the valley's embrace, we laughed aloud.

On a rock, we sat, my sister and me,
Mother's camera clicked, capturing glee.
She painted our joy, a masterpiece bright,
Now with my sister, a cherished delight.

Springtime dances, lighthearted and free,
Floral dresses, lacy socks, joyous glee.
To nature's rhythm, we sway and sing,
In the bloom of spring, life's truest spring.

Sweet November

In November's mist, where shadows play,
Nelson walks, in the chill of the day.
Ambition's chains, his heart entwined,
Till Sara whispers, "I mend hearts, confined."

Sara, a whisper, both gentle and wise,
With eyes that hold secrets, beneath autumn
skies.
In her embrace, Nelson finds release,
From the prison of his longing, sweet peace.

A month's decree, Sara's whispered vow,
"I heal souls," she says, with a solemn brow.
Reluctant at first, Nelson takes flight,
To November's sanctuary, where darkness meets
light.

Their love blooms, like roses in bloom,
In the garden of time, dispelling gloom.
Sweet dances by the shore, moments divine,
With every step, their hearts entwine.

But as November fades, so does her grace,
Revealing truths veiled in the space.
Sara, a fragile rose, fading away,
Leaving Nelson to mourn, in November's gray.

Bench Talks: Tales of Autumn

In autumn's breeze, leaves softly sway,
Golden hues paint the streets each day.
Letting go, like leaves, we find release,
Welcoming change, our hearts at peace.

Amidst the rustle of falling leaves,
We shed old burdens, like autumn trees.
Spring may charm, but autumn's our delight,
A season of growth, in nature's light.

On benches, strangers share a smile,
Conversations warm, even just for a while.
Just as leaves drift, so do we,
In life's dance, embracing what's free.

Rainy Day Escapades

Raindrops surprise, falling from above,
Joy fills hearts, like a flying dove.
Kids dance in puddles, under clouds so gray,
In colorful rain, they find their way.

Snacks at home, a comforting delight,
Rain taps the windows, a cozy night.
The earth's sweet scent, calming all qualms,
Like a soothing song, in nature's arms.

Lightning flashes, anticipation high,
Waiting for thunder, beneath the sky.
But stepping outside, in muddy terrain,
Umbrellas fail, clothes bear the stain.

Cancelled plans, a pleasant measure,
A day at home, simple leisure.
Work and school paused, time to unwind,
In the rain's embrace, peace we find.

Little Explorer's Joyful Day

In a big world, I play every day,
Exploring in my own little way.
Butterflies flutter, birds sing a tune,
In the garden, 'neath the sun's warm boon.

Mom hugs, Dad smiles, fill me with cheer,
Puppy kisses and kitty purrs near.
Rain taps softly, puddles invite,
Jumping in brings pure delight.

At bedtime, stories softly told,
Dreams take flight, as I grow bold.
Oh, to be five, so small and free,
With the world waiting, just for me.

Spin and Strive: A Table Tennis Tale

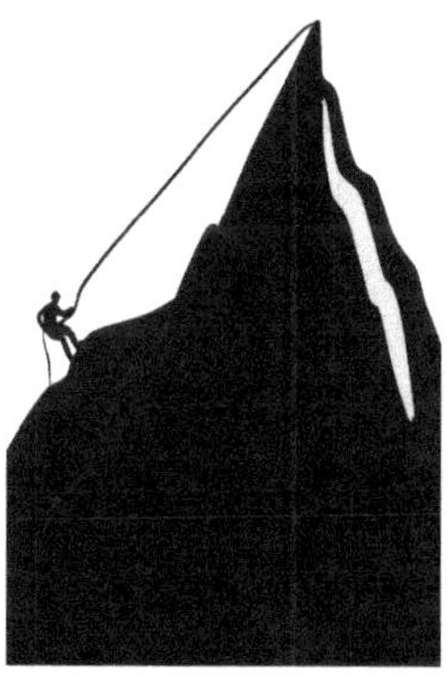

In the arena's hush, with a racket in hand,
I stand, a warrior, on this sacred land.
The table, the net, opponents in my sight,
In table tennis' embrace, I find my light.

With every stroke, emotions collide,
A symphony of effort, my heart open wide.
Backhand, forehand, each shot I send,
In this dance of passion, my soul transcends.

The rhythm of the game, a heartbeat's thrum,
As the ball flies, I'm lost, I'm numb.
Focus sharp, but emotions run deep,
In this whirlwind of challenge, my secrets I
keep.

Each point, a battle, a trial of fire,
I fight with passion, with burning desire.
Victory or defeat, it's all the same,
For on this table, I bare my flame.

In the heat of battle, I find release,
In the whirlwind of motion, I find peace.
Table tennis, my refuge, my sanctuary, my art,
A canvas for emotion, from the depths of my
heart.

Dawn's Embrace: A Symphony of Silence

In the gentle lull of dawn's embrace,
Where the sky meets the horizon in a tender kiss,
I find myself lost in the quiet beauty of the world.

The soft hues of morning paint the landscape,
A canvas of delicate pastels that blend seamlessly,
As if nature herself were a master artist at work.

Birds greet the day with their joyful chorus,
Each note a thread in the rich music of sound,
That weaves through the air, binding earth and sky.

In the distance, a river murmurs its timeless
song,
A melody that speaks of ancient secrets,
Of journeys begun and adventures yet to unfold.

And as I stand in this moment of stillness,
I am reminded of the simple wonder of
existence,
Of the beauty that surrounds us, if only we take
the time to see.

Shimla's Winter Magic

Through tours and travels, to Shimla we went,
With strangers beside, our silence was bent.
Reached the hotel, lunch filled the air,
A game brought us close, bonds began to flare.

Next day to snow valley, with laughter and
cheer,
Snow fights and snowmen, winter's delight
clear.
Snow in my boots, feet freezing and numb,
Snow sickness struck, yet fun had just begun.

I sat on a yak, felt tall and so grand,
Chicken meals grew boring, a change we did
plan.
Dad and uncle brought fish, grilled and divine,
A feast in the mountains, a memory so fine.

At night by the fire, ghost stories we spun,
Me and my cousins, card games were fun.
I won every time, they groaned in dismay,
The only sad part was the end of our stay.
So much joy in Shimla, in my heart it will stay.

Christmas Magic

In the air, a festive cheer,
Families gather, loved ones near.
Trees adorned in lights so bright,
Sparkling with joy, in the night.

Baby Jesus, born in hay,
Three kings came, to him they pray.
A powerful figure, in time he'd be,
Bringing hope to all, setting hearts free.

Children sleep, dreams in their eyes,
Awaiting Santa's grand surprise.
But it's also Mom's special day,
Gifts and cake, in every way.

Morning breaks, with joy we see,
Gifts beneath the Christmas tree.
Streets adorned, with lights aglow,
A wintry scene, a gentle snow.

At midnight's feast, hearts unite,
In warmth and love, the perfect night.
Christmas magic, fills the air,
A season of joy, beyond compare.

New Year's Eve

Plans are made, for the night so bright,
Parties and masquerades, in the moon's soft
light.
As the year's end draws near, we gather 'round,
Celebrating memories lost and new ones found.

Cakes and champagnes, symbols of cheer,
Fireworks burst, making visions clear.
With loved ones near, we bid the old adieu,
Welcoming the new, with hearts renewed.

Candles flicker, as wishes are made,
Silent hopes, in the dark they fade.
A night for endings, and fresh starts anew,
In nostalgia's embrace, we bid fond adieu.

Yet some toil on, in the night's silent grace,
No celebrations, no smiles on their face.
Let's reach out, make them feel less alone,
For in unity's warmth, true joy is shown.

Pride and Prejudice

In Hertfordshire's fields, where whispers play,
Longbourn rests in the light of day.
Elizabeth, a flower in morning's glow,
With laughter and spirit, her beauty aglow.

At Pemberley's halls, Darcy stands tall,
His heart guarded, yet ready to fall.
Beneath his stern gaze, a warmth is found,
In love's gentle whispers, their hearts are bound.

Through society's judgments, they must stride,
In the dance of pride, and love denied.
Yet through misunderstandings, they find,
A love true and kind, in hearts entwined.

In the end, as pride and prejudice fade,
Their love remains a serenade.
In the story of fate, their souls align,
Elizabeth and Darcy, are forever intertwined.

The Pursuit of Happyness: A Symphony of Dreams

In streets of struggle, a father's plight,
With dreams in heart, and stars in sight.
Chris Gardner, with hopes so high,
Faces hardship, with a father's sigh.

From rags, he rises, with his son in tow,
A journey of hardship, yet onward they go.
Through shelter and tears, they face each day,
With grit and determination, come what may.

From homeless nights to corporate halls,
A rags-to-riches tale, as destiny calls.
With dreams as their compass, they journey far,
A bond unbroken, beneath each star.

In pursuit of happiness, they forge their way,
From humble beginnings to brighter days.

Through trials and triumphs, they find their place,
A testament to courage, in life's embrace.

Mahabharata: The Epic of Dharma

In ancient lands, where legends reign,
A battle rages, amidst the pain.
Pandavs and Kauravs, on fields of fate,
A clash of titans, of love and hate.

Arjuna, the warrior, with a bow in hand,
Stands with his brothers, in the righteous stand.
Yet shadows lurk, in Kaurav's hold,
A darkness deep, with tales untold.

Through trials of fire, they fight the fight,
Of virtue and vice, in the dead of night.
Each side is entrenched, in beliefs they hold,
A battle of good vs. evil, stories told.

In history's pages, their tales unfold,
Of battles fought, of stories bold.
Through valor and sacrifice, their destinies are
sealed,
In the epic of Dharma, their fates are revealed.

Structure of Dreams: Verses by a Struggling Architect

Heavy with emotions, I strive to contain,
Behind walls of design, I hide the pain.
Architecture, is not just a career, but a choice made,
In blueprints and sketches, my solace is laid.

Crafting structures not merely for pay,
But to keep the inner storms at bay.
Each edifice is a testament to my strength,
A refuge built from trials, each length.

From towering skyscrapers to humble abodes,
Each building tells tales of joys and woes.
In the concrete, echoes of my own strife,
A reflection of my journey, my life.

Reminiscent of my struggles, I find,
In the concrete, echoes of my mind.
Survival, a battle fought without a nod,
Made the grind, my own god.

The Godfather

In New York, the Corleone family strong,
Michael, the youngest, wants to belong.
He avoids crime, but when his dad's attacked,
He joins the fight, and there's no turning back.

Michael's brother is killed in a feud,
He takes revenge, his soul is subdued.
He plans and schemes, becomes the boss,
But loses his soul, a heavy cost.

In Sicily, he finds his bride,
But she's killed, and he can't hide.
Back in New York, he takes control,
His heart turns cold, he pays the toll.

A baptism scene, calm and grim,
As rivals fall, Michael wins.
Power gained, but family's lost,
A tragic tale, at a great cost.

The Language of Butterflies

In gardens where the flowers bloom,
Butterflies dance in a silent room.
Their wings a palette, colors bright,
A secret language in their flight.

In patterns grand, they weave their tale,
Of nectar sweet and gentle vale.
Each flutter speaks of joy and grace,
In sunlight's warmth, they find their place.

Through meadows green, they whisper low,
Of places where the wild things grow.
In every beat, a message clear,
Of nature's song, so pure and dear.

The secret language, softly told,
In wings of silk, in hues of gold.
Butterflies, in silent cheer,
Speak of beauty, year by year.

The Journey of a Message in a Bottle

Tossed by waves in ocean's sweep,
A bottle floats in secrets deep.
Within, a note of love and plea,
In glass confined, yet roaming free.

Through stormy nights and sunlit days,
It drifts along the ocean's ways.
From distant shore to unknown land,
A message held in fate's own hand.

It speaks of hope, of longing's call,
Of hearts entwined and dreams that fall.
A timeless tale in a bottle kept,
Of tears that fell, of love that leapt.

When found, it tells a story old,
Of love and loss, of words so bold.
A journey vast, in ocean wide,
A message held by time and tide.

The Hidden World of a Bookstore Cat

Among the shelves of tales untold,
A bookstore cat, both shy and bold.
It weaves through aisles with silent grace,
Guarding stories in its space.

With emerald eyes, it watches keen,
The readers lost in a literary scene.
By day it naps in sunlit spots,
By night it roams in quiet plots.

A confidant to every book,
In hidden nooks, it steals a look.
A purr, a stretch, a gentle tread,
Its life among the books is led.

In pages worn, its whiskers brush,
In whispered tales, it finds its hush.
A bookstore cat, a guardian true,
In every story, it finds its due.

The Secret Life of a Circus Tent

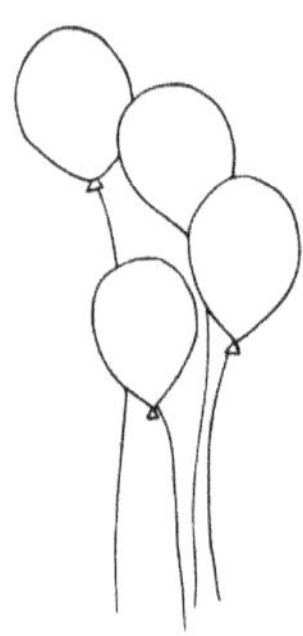

Beneath the stripes of red and gold,
A circus tent's wild tales unfold.
By day, it sleeps in sunlight's gleam,
By night, it's more than what it seems.

Acrobats soar in daring flight,
Lions roar with all their might.
Clowns with laughter fill the air,
In every corner, magic's flair.

The ringmaster's call, a trumpet's blare,
Transform the tent to a world so rare.
Yet in the dawn, when crowds depart,
The tent holds memories in its heart.

A secret life of joy and thrill,
In fabric walls, the dreams distill.
A circus tent, both grand and small,
Holds wonder in its canvas thrall.

The Tales Told by a Street Artist

On city streets where people pass,
A street artist sits with paint and glass.
With every stroke, a story blooms,
Of love and life in vivid rooms.

Murals grand on brick walls spread,
Of dreams and thoughts from an artist's head.
Each passerby, a muse to see,
In colors bright, their lives set free.

In chalk and spray, in brush's grace,
He captures time, he fills the space.
A silent poet in urban scene,
With every piece, a living dream.

Through rain and shine, his art remains,
A testament to joy and pains.
A street artist, with a soul so vast,
In every stroke, a world is cast.

The Chronicles of a Time Traveler's Journal

In leather-bound with pages worn,
A time traveler's journal, stories born.
From future realms to ancient past,
A chronicle of journeys vast.

A scribe of moments lost and found,
Of distant lands and times unbound.
In every page, adventures grand,
A journey through a timeless land.

In scribbled notes and sketches fine,
Of pyramids and coliseums divine.
Of future cities, skies so blue,
A window to what might come true.

The journal holds a universe,
In every line, the cosmos bursts.
A traveler's tale, forever spun,
In ink and paper, journeys done.

Blood-Red eyes

In the school's dim light, she wakes with a start,
Tube lights flicker, casting shadows in her heart.
Down the hallway, a figure calls her name,
Fear grips her tight, like a burning flame.

To the library she flees, seeking refuge there,
A hand covers her mouth, causing despair.
Glasses tumble, revealing a face distorted,
Eyes like rubies, her mind contorted.

A spell is whispered, her thoughts grow hazy,
Blood-red eyes, glaring, almost crazy.
As she succumbs to sleep, the figure fades away,
Leaving her with a ring, in shades of red astray.

She awakens bewildered, with a ring in hand,
A ruby so bright, like a spell unplanned.

Confused and shaken, by the night's strange tale,
In her heart, the memory of those eyes leaves a
lingering trail.

Snowy Nights

By the hearth's warm glow, where firelight
gleams,
A chair and blanket, wrapped in cozy dreams.
Vintage books in hand, lost in pages old,
Winter's best moments, a story told.

Dinners warm and hearty, soups that steam,
Chicken feasts and more, a culinary dream.
The first snow falls, a sight to behold,
Memory's canvas painted white and bold.

Snowmen crafted with care, in the yard they
stand,
Carrot noses, scarves, from mittened hands.
Board games and stories, family gathered tight,
Laughter echoes through the frosty night.

Sweaters, mufflers, gloves, once stored away,
Now embraced with joy, in winter's play.
These are the nights of winter's serene,
Where warmth and love, in every moment seen.

Muted Musings: Words of a Despairing Poet

In the silence, whispers untold,
Mysteries of the cosmos, secrets unfold.
Bridging barriers, breaking every curse,
My pen dances, words undoing the hearse.

A familiar rhythm, a pain ever raw,
Heart's ache, an unending gnaw.
Infinite realms, time's singular chime,
Words evade thoughts in their prime.

Amidst life's canvas, people weave,
Every encounter is a lesson to perceive.
Ink stains paper, tales in my defense,
Yet fleeting, fading in life's expanse.

What brews within, thoughts unspun,
A dance of ideas, yet to be won.
Words, like threads, woven with care,
A tapestry of truth, beyond compare.

The Echoes of an Abandoned Theater

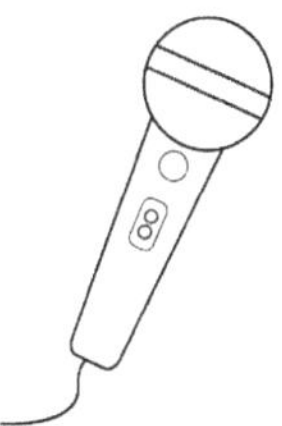

In velvet seats, where crowds once cheered,
Now only shadows have appeared.
Curtains fall on the empty stage,
Where actors danced and singers raged.

The chandelier, in silence, sways,
Reflecting dreams of bygone days.
Ghostly whispers fill the air,
Of stories told with utmost care.

The echo of applause still rings,
In corridors where silence clings.
A phantom audience takes its place,
In every corner, in every space.

Yet in the dust, a spirit gleams,
Of endless plays and timeless dreams.
An empty theater, rich with lore,
In shadows lives forever more.

The Enigma of a Haunted Mansion

Upon a hill, in shadows deep,
A haunted mansion lies asleep.
Its walls hold tales of ghostly lore,
Of whispered cries and creaking floor.

By day, it stands in eerie grace,
By night, it's more than just a place.
Spirits roam in every hall,
In phantom dance, they rise and fall.

A chandelier with flickering light,
Guides lost souls through endless nights.
In mirrors, shadows come to play,
In corners dark, the past holds sway.

The mansion's walls, a silent scream,
Of lives once lived, of broken dreams.
An enigma wrapped in history's thread,
A house alive with the silent dead.

The Quiet Strength of Therapists

Every day they come, with tales of woe,
Grieving, traumatized, emotions aglow.
The therapist listens, it's their daily chore,
But beneath their smile, there's much more.

Underrated heroes, carrying a load,
Vicarious trauma, a heavy road.
Empathetic souls, absorbing the pain,
Their own struggles, hidden in vain.

They stand strong, against the emotional tide,
Guiding others, while their own hearts bide.
For emotional wounds, like stabs in the chest,
Take time to heal, unlike the rest.

The Forgotten Songs of Stars

In night's embrace, the stars do sing,
A cosmic choir, the heavens bring.
Their melodies in silence flow,
A symphony the night does show.

Ancient tunes from distant light,
Whispered secrets in the night.
Each star a note in the vast expanse,
In the universe's endless dance.

Forgotten songs of ages past,
In every star, a memory cast.
They hum of worlds so far away,
Of dreams and hopes, in night's display.

Yet as we gaze in silent awe,
Their music binds us, without flaw.
The stars, they sing, though we may not hear,
Their ancient songs forever near.

The Abyss Within: Poetry of Nihilism and Desolation

In the depths of despair, where shadows reign,
I wander through the abyss, in silent pain.
A Kafkaesque nightmare, surreal and bleak,
Where truth is obscured, and hope is weak.

Dostoevsky's characters tormented and lost,
In the labyrinth of the mind, they pay the cost.
Existential anguish, a weight on the soul,
As Nietzsche's words echo, taking their toll.

The void within, a gaping maw,
Devouring all meaning, leaving me raw.
In the heart of nihilism, I find my home,
Where despair and desolation freely roam.

The absurdity of existence, a cruel jest,
As I confront the void within my chest.
In the silence of despair, I hear the call,
Of darkness and nothingness, consuming all.

But amidst the despair, a flicker of light,
A spark of defiance, in the endless night.
For in the depths of the abyss, I find my voice,
A poet of nihilism, making my choice.

To embrace the void, and stare into the abyss,
To find meaning in meaninglessness, this I vow
to miss.
For in the poetry of despair, there lies a truth,
A truth born from darkness, in the heart of
youth.

Shadows of Disillusionment:
A Politician's Lament

In the corridors of power, I stand,
A puppet in a grand charade,
Promises made, but truth unmanned,
In this game of power, I'm dismayed.

Once filled with fervor, and ideals bright,
I entered the arena with hope untamed,
But the reality of politics, a bitter bite,
Leaving my dreams tarnished and maimed.

Deals struck behind closed doors,
Agendas hidden beneath a veil of lies,
The illusion of democracy, it bores,
As corruption festers and truth dies.

The people's voice, a mere whisper,
Drowned out by greed and self-interest,
In this pool of deceit, I wither,
A disillusioned politician, morally bereft.

Yet still, I cling to a glimmer of hope,
That one day, integrity will prevail,
That the broken system will find a scope,
For justice to reign and truth to unveil.

Reality's Mirage: Hallucinations of a VR Gamer

Beneath the veil of my VR headset's glow,
I find respite from life's relentless flow.
Is this escape a facade or my true domain?
In the digital realm, do I truly remain?

Alone in my sanctuary of screens and codes,
Online companions, pixels, and nodes.
Yet amidst the pixels, emotions do dwell,
In this virtual world, do I bid reality farewell?

The obsession grows, blurring lines once clear,
Lost in the labyrinth of what's virtual and near.
As the screen dims, night's shadows creep,
Reality's whispers stir from their sleep.

In the quiet hours, when screens fade to black,
I'm left grappling with what I lack.
Reality's hues, muted yet true,
Calls me back from the digital hue.

Solitary Struggles: Weathering Parenthood Alone

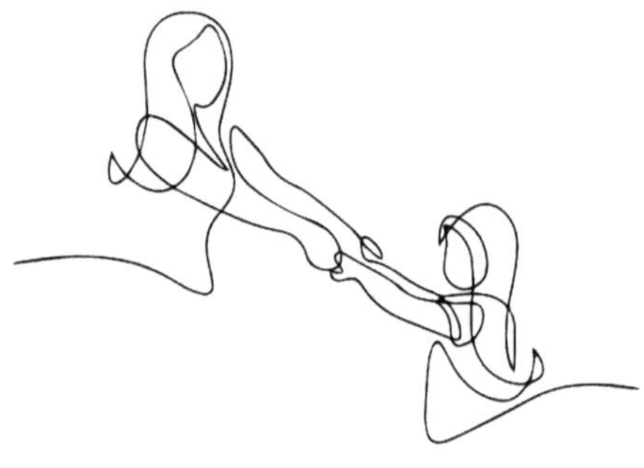

In the silence before dawn, I rise, weary yet determined,
A single parent, navigating a world uncertain,
Each day a battle, every moment a test,
Balancing responsibilities, and striving to do my best.

The weight of the world rests heavily on my shoulders,
Juggling roles, dreams, and unspoken boulders.
In the depths of exhaustion, I find my way,
Guiding my children through life's disarray.

The nights are long, the days even longer,
Yet in their laughter, I find the strength to grow
stronger.
For every sacrifice, every tear I shed,
Is a testament to the love, the life we've led.

Through storms and struggles, we press on,
Bound together by love, though the path seems
long.
Though the journey is rough, and the road
unclear,
We march forward, fueled by hope and the love
we hold dear.

The Symphony of Forgotten Toys

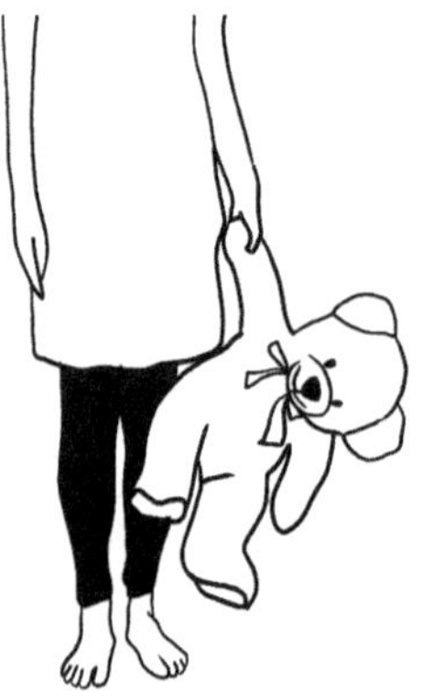

In dusty attic, shadows play,
Forgotten toys from yesterday.
Each one holds a child's delight,
Now silent in the soft moonlight.

A teddy bear with buttoned eyes,
Remembers hugs and lullabies.
A wooden train once full of cheer,
Now rests alone, year after year.

A music box with broken tune,
Still whispers dreams beneath the moon.
Dolls and soldiers, games once grand,
Now gather dust, by time's command.

In every toy, a memory,
Of childhood's bright and boundless sea.
A symphony of laughter past,
In silent echoes, forever cast.

The Memoirs of a Forgotten Astronaut

In silence deep, beyond the sky,
An astronaut's dreams still fly.
Through endless space, where stars ignite,
He journeys on in cosmic night.

Forgotten now, his tales unsung,
In the void of space, his heart has clung.
To distant worlds and moons so cold,
His legacy in silence told.

Among the stars, his spirit roams,
In cosmic winds, he finds his home.
A lone explorer, brave and true,
His story etched in starlit blue.

In galaxies, his name will shine,
A testament to humankind.
A forgotten hero, lost in space,
Yet ever bound by endless grace.

The Great Gatsby

In shadows cast, Gatsby, a figure veiled,
Mysterious, and elusive, his secrets sailed.
Through lavish balls, he spun a grand facade,
But behind the affluence, a longing gnawed.

From his port, he stared across the bay,
Dreams drifting with the tides, day by day.
Daisy's words, a haunting refrain,
"All the bright, precious things fade in vain."

Each festivity, a silent plea,
For Daisy's return, his heart to free.
But in the glittering swirl of champagne and
delight,
Gatsby found solace in the darkest of the night.

Yet, beneath the veneer of wealth and desire,
Lay a truth untold, a love's funeral prayer.
In the end, amidst whispers and strife,
Gatsby's dreams dissolved in the sands of life.

One Minute-Time Machine

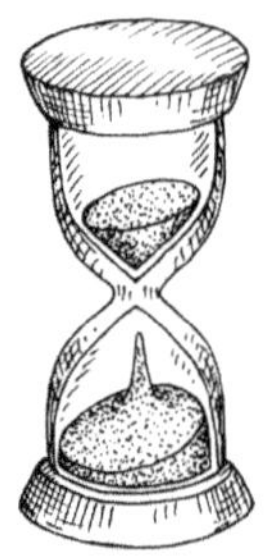

James, a scientist, with a heart's desire,
Builds a time machine, with hopes afire.
One minute passed, and he took his chance,
To win her heart, in a fleeting glance.

But fate's cruel jest, in time's cruel play,
Resets the clock, with each dismay.
Again he tries, in an endless loop,
To break the cycle, in lover's troupe.

Through laughter and tears, he seeks the key,
To unlock the mystery, in time's decree.
Yet in the end, in one minute's span,
A loop unbroken, in time's grand plan.

In echoes of time, he's trapped in rhyme,
A lover's pursuit, through endless time.
In each fleeting moment, a chance to find,
Echoes of time's dance, in lover's bind.

A Walk with Questions

A man walked in thought, through paths serene,
Pondering God and what belief might mean.
Why do people seek a higher grace?
Is it hope in distress, or life's embrace?

Some claim they see the supernatural's might,
Cult worship and possessions in the night.
If darkness exists, must goodness be near?
Newton's law suggests balance is clear.

Yet, he saw rituals, traditions held dear,
Money and effort, it all seemed unclear.
Milk to a statue, down gutters it streamed,
A poor man collecting, a sorrowful scene.

Why not tend to God's children with care?
Feed the hungry, show love everywhere.
The Almighty, needing nothing of our gain,
Yet humans, flawed, in rituals remain.

The Reality of Having Siblings

In the beginning, so small and sweet,
Older sibling's heart skips a beat.
They giggle and play, a bond so pure,
Every laugh and smile, they adore.

As years roll by, the quarrels start,
Over chocolates, clothes, a tug-of-heart.
Wrestling matches, tantrums flare,
But when scolded, they become a pair.

When fast food's the prize, they plot and
scheme,
Convincing Mom and Dad, a dream team.
Rivalries fade, they join forces tight,
Victory's delicious, the meal just right.

In tough times, they stand hand in hand,
Whispering secrets, a close-knit band.
Older's a guide, firm yet kind,
Younger's the jester, always on their mind.
Together they laugh, the perfect crew,
With playful antics, there's nothing they can't
do.

Aged Perspectives

In the twilight of my days, I stand,
Life's journey traced in lines and bends.
Memories flicker, stories told,
In quiet moments, both young and old.

Each wrinkle a tale, each ache a sign,
Of days gone by, of moments fine.
The world has changed, I've seen it all,
But love and gratitude still stand tall.

Clock ticks slower, days slip away,
Yet in my heart, a steady sway.
For every laugh, for every tear,
Grateful for the journey, far and near.

Bound by Age, Free in Spirit

In my days of youth, I danced with grace,
Each step a joy, each moment a race,
Now frail and weak, I dream once more,
Of running free on life's bright shore.

Once hands so strong, could build and mend,
Now tremble weak, on others depend,
To eat, to walk, such tasks a strain,
Oh, to be young and whole again.

Memories of laughter, boundless skies,
Now in my bed, I close my eyes,
And wish for days when I was free,
Not bound by age's cruel decree.

Yet in my heart, a spark remains,
A youthful spirit, despite the pains,
To live again, to soar, to strive,
Beyond this bed, to feel alive.

Echoes of Empathy: A Social Worker's Anthem

In eyes weighed by despair, shadows linger,
Unseen struggles, silent cries, fingers tremor.
Clothes threadbare, hunger gnaws, woes untold,
In the realm of the forgotten, hearts grow cold.

Within me, a yearning to mend and bestow,
To share their load, sow seeds of hope to sow.
In sorrow's depths, I offer a listening ear,
A beacon of empathy, a sanctuary near.

With outstretched hands, I offer my embrace,
Feeling their pain, in the quietest space.
Together, we seek a brighter sunrise,
In unity, hope and empathy arise.

In the symphony of souls, hearts entwine,
Building castles from whispers divine.
With every step, we light up the dark,
In compassion's embrace, we ignite a spark.

Pragmatic Positivity: Outlook of a Realistic Optimist

Maintaining cheer is quite the task,
Especially when shadows seem to bask.
Yet I seek the glimmer in each plight,
To imbue my day with radiant light.

Navigating hardships is no simple feat,
And optimism can sometimes seem obsolete.
Yet within the realm of choice, we dwell,
To embrace confidence or let sorrow swell.

Neither dictates the path we take,
But they do sculpt our present's stake.
We're tasked to choose, to suffer or soar,
To kindle joy or let anguish roar.

Though dark clouds may obscure our view,
And tears may trickle, a storm to ensue.
But when joy's tender embrace draws near,
Let's smile, let's shine, without fear.

The Timekeeper's Melody: The Adventures of a Time Traveler

Navigating through the currents of time,
A mere observer of the flow of history,
Defiance of nature, indeed an act of crime,
Daunting and exciting, this is my story.

With great power comes great responsibility,
Bound by laws of causality,
Every decision I make,
Has the potential to change the course of history,
A small alteration could change the fabric of
reality.

Yet, amidst time's complexities,
There is beauty to be found, many reveries,

May it be the resilience of humans during war,
Or the aristocracy's lavish balls,
I witness them all.

I am a guardian of knowledge,
Carrying the stories of countless generations,
Embracing adventure at every step,
And all of the universe's creations.

Whispers of the Unknown: The Melancholy of a Mythical Creature in Hiding

In solitude's embrace, I find my rest,
Amidst winds' whispers and leaves' soft caress,
Once hailed as a legend, now cast to roam,
In lands unknown, where shadows find their
home.

Once free to roam, in magic's sweet embrace,
Our beauty sung in tales, our glory traced.
But mortal hearts, with fear and mistrust,
Drove us to exile, where shadows clutch.

Alone I tread, in forests' solemn sigh,
And marshes forsaken 'neath the moonlit sky.
Yet even in exile, beauty does bloom,
In mountains' majesty and starlit gloom.

So I wander on, a spirit unbroken,
Seeking solace in nature's soft-spoken.
For though in exile, my heart finds its home,
In echoes of ancient songs, I'm not alone.

Fading Light: A Cancer Patient's Reflection

In sterile halls where shadows dance,
I lie upon a bed of chance.
The whispers of machines, the scent of fear,
Echoes of sorrow, drawing near.

Beneath fluorescent lights that flicker low,
I count the moments as they go.
Each tick of the clock is a reminder stark,
Of the fragile thread that holds my heart.

The cold touch of metal, the sting of pain,
A relentless battle fought in vain.
But in the depths of despair, a glimmer of light,
A fleeting hope, burning bright.

For in the twilight of my days,
I choose to dance amidst the haze.
To seize each moment, to breathe each breath,
To embrace the beauty in life and death.

With every sunrise, a promise anew,
To cherish the moments, both old and new.
For though my time may soon be done,
My spirit will live on, forever spun.

So let the tears fall, let the sorrow fade,
For, in the end, love will never fade.
And though my journey may soon end,
I'll live each moment, until the very end.

In Search of Tomorrow: A Teenage Runaway Story

In the dead of night, I quietly slip away,
Seeking freedom's solace, in the moon's soft
sway.
Every stranger I pass, a potential ally or threat,
In the urban labyrinth, where fears and hopes
intersect.

Away from home's shelter, criticisms sting and
bite,
Yet I press on, driven by a restless fight.
The road ahead, fraught with shadows and fears,
Each step forward is a testament to my silent
tears.

A teenage runaway, in search of a distant shore,
A rebel without a cause, seeking something
more.

Through the chaos of the city, I find my voice,
Navigating the darkness, making my own
choice.

In the stillness of the night, I find my stride,
Embracing the unknown, with courage as my
guide.
For though the path is daunting, and the future
unclear,
I walk with purpose, knowing freedom draws
near.

Beyond Borders: A Tale of Cross-Cultural Love

In the vast expanse of digital space, where
connections ignite,
A love story unfolds transcending distance's
plight.
She, amidst the vibrant energy of city streets,
He is in the rhythm of urban life, where dreams
meet.

Across screens and time zones, their love takes
flight,
In virtual embraces, they find their delight.
Through messages and calls, they bridge the
divide,
Each moment was cherished, on this
long-distance ride.

Navigating cultures, they learn and grow,
In the ebb and flow of love's gentle flow.
With patience and understanding, they find their
way,
Through the challenges of distance, day by day.

In the quiet hours, when screens glow in the
night,
They dream of a future bathed in love's light.
For in the tapestry of their cross-cultural bond,
Distance is but a challenge, not a magic wand.

Together, they find strength in the space
between,
Knowing that love conquers all, serene.
In the dance of their relationship, they find their
grace,
Navigating long-distance with love as their
embrace.

Trysts Beneath the Stars: Serendipity's Embrace

Shall we dance once more beneath the moon's
sway?
An unexpected meeting, fate's playful play.
His eyes, a mesmerizing trance, a spark,
Yet shadowed by past scars, the light grows
stark.

Do I dare desire what he flaunts?
His words a playful dance, his jests and haunts.
Still, amidst the banter, I find solace heard,
In his touch, a revelation, a whispered word.

A single touch, a world anew,
A budding love, a promise, a debut.
In his embrace, a symphony sings,
Love's melody, how sweetly it rings.

Healing each other's broken parts,
In the dance of love, where healing starts.
A bond forged, forever to weather,
In each other's arms, always together.

The Ghost of Love: Poetry of Faded Affection

Amidst the whispers of the trees, echoes of the past,
I seek your shadow in the breeze, hoping it will last.
Yet the path to you stretches, seemingly without end,
For in your absence, I cannot pretend.

Days drift by, tinged with a silent regret,
Gazing at the sky, memories I cannot forget.
The bond we forged, now faded, yet still strong,
A bittersweet melody, an unfinished song.

Is happiness a fleeting dream, a fragile thing?
In the depths of longing, echoes of a forgotten spring.

Yet I believe in the promise of a brighter day,
Where faded memories find solace, and pain
fades away.

Time, they say, heals all wounds with gentle
grace,
Like a hearth's warm embrace, in its comforting
space.
As the fire crackles, memories flicker and
gleam,
In the quiet moments, love remains a silent
dream.

Petals of Longing: A Tale of Unrequited Love

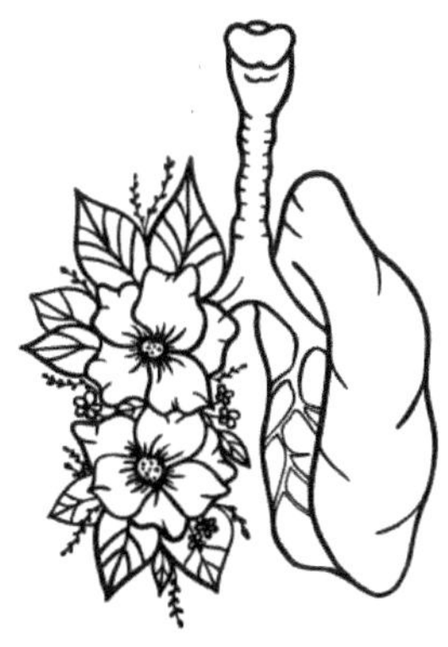

In the stillness of the night, I yearn,
Gathering shattered pieces, desperate to learn.
Why our love faltered, what went awry,
Aching for answers beneath the starlit sky.

A heaviness weighs upon my chest,
Each breath is a struggle, each heartbeat a test.
You, once a conquest, now a haunting specter,
Leaving me tangled in this love's cruel vector.

Alone in darkness, the ceiling my solace,
Lost in the labyrinth of love's remorse.
Pain and agony, a relentless haze,
Enveloping me in its suffocating embrace.

Each cough, a petal falls, a sign,
Of the Hanahaki's curse, a silent shrine.
As I drown in petals, consumed by despair,
I grasp for redemption, a fleeting prayer.

Oh, how I long for your reciprocated yearn,
For you to see, to finally discern.
That my love for you, deeper than the sea,
Is a plea for salvation, a desperate plea.

In the depths of unrequited affection, I pine,
Praying for love's return, for a lifeline divine.
For without your love, I wither and fade,
A victim of love's curse, in this tragic charade.

Lost Stardom: The Legacy of a Child Prodigy

In the glare of the spotlight, I once stood tall,
A child of wonder, destined to enthrall.
With every accolade, my star did rise,
A prodigy in the world's searching eyes.

But behind the facade of success, I bore,
The weight of expectation, a heavy lore.
Each achievement is a burden to bear,
In the relentless pursuit of perfection, I lost my share.

Childhood dreams sacrificed on the altar of
fame,
A relentless drive, an unquenchable flame.
Yet with every triumph, a piece of me died,
As I chased shadows, longing to find.

Now, a former prodigy, lost in the crowd,
Haunted by memories, both silent and loud.
Yearning for simplicity, for a life unknown,
To reclaim the innocence, the joy I once owned.

Yet amidst the ruins of shattered dreams,
A flicker of hope, a distant gleam.
For in the quiet moments, I find solace anew,
Embracing the journey, and rediscovering what
is true.

Battles of the Mind: Poetic Resilience in the Face of PTSD

In the stillness of the night, I hear them call,
Echoes of trauma, haunting in their sprawl.
Nightmares grip me in their relentless hold,
A prisoner of memory, trapped in stories untold.

Flashbacks pierce the silence, vivid and raw,
Visions of horror, a relentless claw.
Every sound, every sight, a trigger to the past,
As I navigate a world that feels like glass.

Anxiety grips me, a vice around my chest,
Each breath is a struggle, a desperate quest.
The weight of fear, a burden I bear,
In the darkness of my mind, it's always there.

Yet amidst the chaos, a glimmer of light,
A ray of hope, pushing back the night.
With each step forward, I reclaim my ground,
A warrior rising, in the battleground.

Cosmic Rhapsody: A Symphony of Transcendental Being

In realms beyond mortal sight, I dwell,
A transcendental being, in an ethereal spell.
Whispering winds, they dance with grace,
As I roam the cosmos, in boundless space.

I am the shimmering light in twilight's embrace,
The essence of stars, in celestial race.
Mountains bow in reverence, rivers sigh,
As I paint the heavens with hues of sky.

Iridescent dreams, they weave and twine,
In the tapestry of time, a dance divine.
I am the echo of eternity's call,
In the silence of galaxies, I stand tall.

With each breath of dawn, a symphony unfurls,
As I traverse the cosmos, in cosmic swirls.
I am the melody of the universe's song,
In the heart of creation, where souls belong.

For I am the essence of all that is seen,
In the dance of existence, forever serene.
A transcendent being, in timeless grace,
Lost in the beauty of infinite space.

The Mind's Odyssey:
Homage to Literary Titans

In the labyrinth of words, where minds collide,
Where Kafka's tales of absurdity reside,
Dostoevsky's characters dance in the night,
Plath's verses echo with darkness and light.
Nietzsche's philosophies challenge and provoke,
While Camus questions life's absurdity cloak.

Kafka, the master of surreal dreams,
In his world, reality seams,
Unravel into chaos, a maze untamed,
Where truth and illusion are forever maimed.

Dostoevsky, the explorer of the human psyche,
In his characters, the depth we spy,
Crime and punishment, guilt and remorse,
In his pages, human nature's discourse.

Plath, the poetess of melancholy,
In her words, the soul's folly,
A mirror to her inner turmoil and strife,
In her verses, the agony of life.

Nietzsche, the thinker of eternal recurrence,
In his aphorisms, the cosmic dance,
Of will to power and the Übermensch,
In his writings, the quest for transcendence.

Camus, the philosopher of the absurd,
In his essays, the silence heard,
Of Sisyphus and his futile boulder,
In his musings, life's absurd order.

In the tapestry of literary lore,
These voices resonate forevermore,
Kafka, Dostoevsky, Plath, Nietzsche, Camus,
In their words, humanity finds its muse.

Eternal Wisdom: Tale of the Reincarnated Sage

In the ebb and flow of time's endless tide,
I am reborn, a vessel of wisdom, wide.
Memories of eras past, stir within,
As I traverse the realms, where truths begin.

Through the veil of illusion, I perceive,
The secrets of existence, I do believe.
For I am the oracle, ancient and wise,
In the dance of fate, where destiny lies.

With each incarnation, I carry the flame,
Of knowledge eternal, beyond the mortal frame.
I see the patterns, the threads of fate,
Woven in the tapestry, of life's debate.

I am the voice of the cosmos, serene and clear,
Guiding souls through the labyrinth of fear.
In the depths of uncertainty, I am the light,
A beacon of hope, in the darkest night.

For I am the oracle, bound to no time,
In the realm of the divine, I do climb.
Through cycles of birth and rebirth, I ascend,
A sage of ages, until time's final end.

From Student to Savior: Spider Verses

In the heart of Queens, where streets align,
A student's tale begins, an ordinary life so fine.
Young Peter Parker, with dreams to ignite,
A nerd with glasses, not yet ready for the fight.

A field trip gone awry, a bite from a spider,
Changed his fate forever, and filled him with
desire.
Powers surged within, strength beyond compare,
But with it came responsibility, a burden to bear.

Uncle Ben's words echoed, "With great power comes great responsibility,"
Guiding Peter's path, shaping his identity.
As tragedy struck, his uncle's life was cut short,
A lesson learned, a promise made, a hero to exhort.

Through skyscrapers he soared, in a suit of red and blue,
A symbol of hope, in a world askew.
With each villain vanquished, each crisis averted,
Peter Parker stood tall, his purpose asserted.

From New York's bustling streets to the far reaches of space,
He fought for justice, in every time and place.
A hero not for fame, but for the greater good,
A beacon of light, where darkness once stood.

So let the world remember, the tale of Peter Parker's might,
A student turned hero, in the blink of a night.
For in his sacrifice, his courage unfurled,
He saved not just a city, but the entire world.

Vines of Valor: Jack's Triumph Over Giants

In a village poor, where dreams lay bare,
Lived Jack, with naught to spare.
An old man, with a gift profound,
Bestowed a bean, in hopes unbound.

Through stormy skies, his house did rise,
To meet the clouds, a wondrous surprise.
Giants descended, hunger in their eyes,
But Jack stood firm, to their surprise.

With courage bold, he sought the crown,
To calm the giants, bring peace down.
Through trials dire, he pressed on true,
Till victory claimed, and darkness flew.

In legend's lore, his name resounds,
Jack the Giant Slayer, courage unbound.
From pauper's plight to hero's grace,
His journey etched, in time's embrace.

The Sixth Sense

In shadows deep, where spirits roam,
A therapist lost, seeking a home.
His footsteps echo in the dark,
As whispers of the past leave their mark.

Dr. Malcolm Crowe, a man of skill,
With secrets buried, his heart lies still.
He meets a boy, with eyes so old,
Who sees the dead, their stories are untold.

Cole Sear, the boy with fears untamed,
Haunted by ghosts, his spirit maimed.
He shares his truth with whispered breaths,
A burden heavy, a dance with death.

But hush, the truth, concealed in gloom,
As the therapist unravels, senses loom.
A chilling whisper, truth's cruel jest,
Reveals the boy's truth, laid to rest.

Malcolm, bewildered, in disbelief,
His reality shattered, beyond relief.
A ghostly revelation, a truth profound,
In silent gaze, redemption's sound.

Yet in this twist, a depth untold,
Memories engulf him as he begs for help,
Knowing that he was a ghost himself.
Echoes of revelation, in shadows bold.

500 Days of Summer

In echoes of memory, a tale is spun,
Of love's sweet dance, beneath the sun.
Tom Hansen, with dreams so high,
Falls for Summer, beneath the sky.

But listen close, to whispers faint,
For truth's reflection, is never quaint.
Summer's side, in shadows cast,
A narrative blurred, from first to last.

Through rose-tinted glasses, Tom recalls,
A love unrequited, as the curtain falls.
But truth's elusive, in summer's glow,
A tale of two hearts, in ebb and flow.

In echoes of memory, the truth resounds,
A story untold, in narrative bounds.
Of love's bitter sting, and hearts that break,
Whispers of heartbreak, in love's wake.

Sun-Kissed Days

Beneath the golden sun, the beaches gleam,
Families gather, a vibrant summer theme.
Children ride waves, their laughter a song,
Ice cream and sundaes, where hearts belong.

For those without shores, pools are the retreat,
Cooling off in splashes, a simple treat.
Indoors we bask in the fans' gentle grace,
Air conditioners hum, a cooling embrace.

Nights are a challenge, sleep's hard to find,
Tossing and turning, heat on our mind.
We scoot under fans, seek solace in air,
In the stillness, sweet dreams, we all share.

Power cuts strike, chaos, world's end it seems,
Yet vacations keep us chasing our dreams.

Trips with friends and family, laughter and
cheer,
Summer's bright magic, the best time of year.

Tiny Feet, Kick and Cry

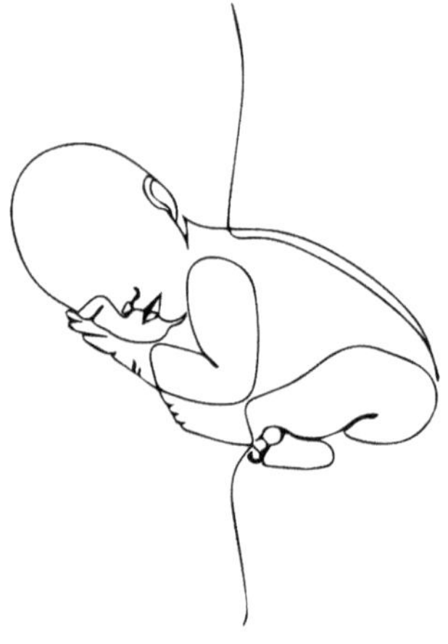

In a world so bright, I open my eyes,
Faces all around, such a big surprise.
Doctors and lights, oh what a sight,
Covered in red, I cry with all my might.

Nurse cleans me up, gentle and kind,
Home we go, leaving the bustle behind.
Smiles and laughter, I'm the star of the show,
Do I look funny? I really don't know!

Warm milk in my tummy, cozy and sweet,
Diapers need changing, oh what a feat!
Playtime is fun, but changing? No way,
Silly faces they make, brighten my day.

At night, Mommy sings, her lullaby soft,
Crib with soft sounds, gentle and aloft.
Crystals that sparkle, teddies so near,
In this warm, loving world, I have nothing to
fear.

Whispers of the Night: Echoes of Ichiko Aoba

In the whispering wind, a tale unfolds,
Of shadows dancing, in moonlight cold.
Echoes of a forgotten song,
In the quiet night, where dreams belong.

Through fields of gold, I wander alone,
In search of solace, a place to call home.
The fragrance of flowers, a memory dear,
As I walk this path, year after year.

Beneath the starry sky, I find my way,
In the gentle glow, where darkness fades away.
The melody of time, a gentle stream,
In the stillness of night, where hopes gleam.

Oh, to wander, lost in reverie,
In the depths of my soul, where truth lies free.
Ichiko's voice, a guiding light,
In the silence of night, where dreams take flight.

Through words unspoken, I find release,
In the beauty of nature, a sense of peace.
With each breath, a new beginning,
In the quietude of night, where stars are singing.

The Land of God

We boarded the flight under night's embrace,
City lights below, like stars in their place.
Irony shines, stars hidden from sight,
As we soar above in the velvety night.

We land and are greeted by a dancer's grace,
A Kathakali artist, with a garland to place.
Welcome to Kerala, where dreams come alive,
In this land of culture, we truly arrive.

Hotel delights with South Indian fare,
Torch and sword show, magic fills the air.
Next day, tea valleys, lush and grand,
Local shopping, treasures in hand.

Christmas in Kerala, a cake we share,
Spas to relax, billiards with flair.
Boat house adventure, lake so serene,
Under clear skies, a cherished dream.

The Shawshank Redemption

Andy, jailed for a crime not done,
In Shawshank, his life begun.
He meets Red, they form a bond,
In prison walls, their hope is strong.

Andy builds a library, helps fellow men,
He plans escape with careful pen.
Years go by, he digs a way,
To freedom's light, a brighter day.

He exposes the warden's evil scheme,
Then escapes through a sewer's stream.
He reaches freedom, finds the sea,
Red follows later, both are free.

Hope and friendship, themes so bright,
In darkest place, they find the light.
Andy's tale, a journey long,
Of freedom found, where hearts belong.

Schindler's List

Oskar Schindler, a businessman shrewd,
In World War II, his conscience renewed.
He saves Jews from the Nazi's grasp,
His factory, their hope to clasp.

He starts for profit, but sees the pain,
Innocent lives, their loss his gain.
He makes a list, a lifeline dear,
To save them from the camps they fear.

A girl in red, a haunting sight,
Inspires Oskar to do what's right.
He spends his wealth, their lives to save,
In darkest times, he's brave.

When war ends, he's mournful, sad,
Wishing he'd saved more with all he had.
A savior in a time so bleak,
Schindler's heart, the tale we speak.

Forrest Gump

Forrest, simple, kind, and true,
Through history's events, his journey grew.
From football star to Vietnam,
He lived a life, a unique plan.

He runs across the country wide,
Meets presidents, and takes it in stride.
He loves Jenny, his heart's one aim,
Through ups and downs, his love remains.

Shrimp boat captain, he finds success,
Loses friends, but still feels blessed.
A son he meets, love so strong,
Forrest's heart, where he belongs.

Through all of life, he stands tall,
A pure heart in spite of it all.
Forrest's tale, a gentle song,
Of love and life, where he belongs.

The Dark Knight

In Gotham City, crime does thrive,
Batman fights to keep it alive.
The Joker rises, chaos reigns,
Batman faces moral strains.

Harvey Dent, a hero bright,
Falls to darkness, loses light.
Rachel's gone, Bruce feels the pain,
Joker's games drive him insane.

Interrogation, Joker's plan,
Tests the limits of Batman.
Good and evil, lines are blurred,
In Gotham's night, hope is stirred.

Batman takes the blame, stands alone,
To protect the city he calls home.
A dark knight's tale, of sacrifice,
In shadows deep, he pays the price.

Titanic

On a grand ship, Rose feels trapped,
Jack, a poor artist, her heart is tapped.
Their love blooms, against the tide,
But disaster looms, and they can't hide.

An iceberg strikes, the ship's in peril,
Their love's tested, in the cruel whirl.
Lifeboats lower, but Jack must stay,
As Titanic sinks, he fades away.

At the bow, arms spread wide,
Their love's proclaimed, against the tide.
In icy waters, Jack lets go,
Rose survives, their story's glow.

Years later, she tells the tale,
Of love and loss, against the gale.
Titanic's fate, a tragic night,
Love's memory, still burns bright.

Inception

Dom Cobb, a thief of dreams,
Steals secrets from subconscious streams.
A final job, to plant a seed,
In a target's mind, an idea's creed.

Layers deep, in dreams they dive,
To make the thought, come alive.
A spinning top, reality's check,
In mind's maze, they find the wreck.

In zero gravity, they fight,
Inception's goal, to set things right.
A wife's lost love, a past's regret,
In dreams they chase, they can't forget.

Success achieved, but doubt remains,
Is it real, or mind's refrains?
The top spins on, reality bends,
In dreams and life, where truth suspends.

Mom and Dad

Dad's hands are calloused, from workday's
grind,
Yet he greets each evening with peace of mind.
Playing cards, his laughter fills the room,
In the game of life, he's mastered every move.

With takeout menus, he's the master of charm,
Teaming up with a wink, keeping hunger at bay
and harm.
He knows our favorites, orders with a flair,
Bringing joy to our table, showing he cares.

Mom's voice, a melody, though stern in her plea,
"Clean your room!" echoes, her persistent
decree.
She frowns at the takeout, preferring
home-cooked delight,
Yet her love is a beacon, shining ever so bright.

In every scold, there's a whisper of care,
In every hug, a promise is always there.
Together they're a duo, the best we've known,
In their warmth and guidance, love's truly
shown.

www.ingramcontent.com/pod-product-compliance
Lightning Source LLC
LaVergne TN
LVHW050909200726

843508LV00011B/2158